INSOMNIA OF A LITTLE GIRL

Journey of Death, Healing, & Rebirth

ELW (A-CHENT)

Phoenix Publishing House, LLC

Publishers since 2016

P.O. BOX 154855

Lufkin, TX 75904

www.phoenixpubllc.com

Copyright ©2021 by ELW (A-CHENT).

Printed in the United States of America

ISBN: 978-1-955235-08-2

Table of Contents

Trauma

<u>Little Trauma (Rest Well)</u>

Dear Little Girl
Lying there in bed
Gazing out the window
Looking at the stars ahead
Your mind racing, thinking,
Does God exist out there?
If you created me,
I must dare to believe you care.
Constant questions lingering like,
What is my destiny?
How will I matter?
Seeking an answer
Then anger entered the heart
Overextended causing many challenges.
Life starts to shatter.
Confused
Trapped
Misunderstood
Battles of trauma with rivals
Love not received the same way its giving.
Bitterness from disappointment

Bruised from shame.
Soon words became sanity.

Reclaiming my name
As you allow them to flow
Enter a space now clear.
The flame lit now burns urgently.
Fear kept you hungry and cold.
Now that stability is at your core.
Dreams become vivid once more.
Little girl
Little girl
So sweet
Beautiful
Innocent
Unique
Full of life
You and I are the same.
I release you to rest.
On your new pillow of change
YOU ARE FREE!

Inner-Twined

Pain, it haunts me
Creeping around like a maniac stalking
Deep inside evolving
Pushing me around like a bully
Crushing my chest so heavy
Crown tilted with thorns
Voice restricted
Heart scorned.
Head cloudy from the storm
Pressure caressing my chin.
Provoking fear from the bottomless pit
The strength ripping the veins
Water murky and smeared.
Caught in the clutch of its grip.
Destined to take a sip.

<u>Which way is Reality?</u>

Laying here with sincere emotions
Just hoping
That one-day love will be free flowing
Maybe it's worthless.
Killer instincts provoking
Moments of pleasure spent bonding with focus
Hoping we won't ultimately face malfunction
Another minute is not promised.
Why do we press rewind glitching for a sign?
Our soul auto erases for time from time
Illusions are resumed to project blank screens.
Never shy away from the truth be devoted, it's cool
They take for granted your purpose according to the creator.
Your position in the kingdom is gatekeeper.
Constantly patient
Riding in the shadows of fail connections.
Distant placement
Picking opponents
Malicious intent
Aggravated
Yet, painting pictures from depictions
Restore your vision.

<u>Be Still</u>

A shift is detected so unexpectedly.
Ripping down the seams or so it seems
Projecting time so innocently
This introspective displays synergy into dark cycles that seep
Actions falsely counted until they fade from the scene
Facing the path of neglect
Breeding confusion into hearts of slumber
No direction to obey
Lost in summer's decay
Building false drama to stage
Roll up and smoke karma
Bashing love from the pain
Missing vital signs speaking words to find likeminded kind
Be still and capture the rain from the peak of the day
Let it cleanse you

<u>Why Do You Hide?</u>

If they call you by your name
Do you answer them the same?
While shifting through chambers of change
Mentally decompressing the shame
Mastering intercession to pray
Pulling the strings of the left vessel unrestrainted.
Gazing back down the path until it's in the distance
Give the ability to show more.
Exist!

In Between

Throwing tantrums seeking domination
Affects the innocence of little faces observing
Crawl deep through bounding spaces
Burdens carried bleed heavy in spring
Matters buried eventually erupt aggressively
Birth defects develop from lack of fear
We move slow from lack to steer
Crave medals like birds snatch worms at dawn
Carried out by infantile dreams
Watching the ship sail from the dock in between

Temple Pressure

Words travel through channels of synthesis.
Boasting hope high like a mantel
Behind the crooked door defeats are cancelled
Counting time in frequency
Bodies laid sideways pillars standing look in daze.
Running from position to labels.
Day to day clearing the wreckage.
Stand still until it turns into passion.

<u>Judgment</u>

When you open those lips to speak harsh
Words spew never bypass they sharp.
Quick to establish boundaries.
Cut from a different cloth indeed.
Deep stench like moth balls ringing the alarm
So cold
Hearts shed strings in sync.
Boiling water burns like heat rising 10 degrees.
Sinking shifts until sanction is reclaimed
Dreams scatter like waves clashing at bay
Kicking piles over just to pretend
That we should all be the same

<u>Starving to See</u>

Little square box
We click on your topic of discussion.
Starving to feast for purpose
With every scroll and mention
Applying filters for perfection.
Letting the world see our confessions.
Obsessed with vast connections.
Craving attention like merchandise on window mannequins.
We are addicted to the game, fanatics
Seeking thrills through unnecessary malice
We are afraid to not to be mentioned.

The Web (Black Widow)

Every time I find peace trying to live it up.
In comes drama just to overeact
Head over heels in love with doom
Cyclones hovering the room.
Death to toxic attraction
Breed new life its fertile ground
Planted deep like pentacles.
Touch and agree like hands to the sky.
Hidden agendas reveal the why
We speak names in silence from shame.
Then sing melodies for praise
Just to be a name
What does it mean to be good?
What line can define perfection?
Borderline is this perception
Craving a taste more like obsessive

Uneven Pages

Never on the same page
One always delayed.
Seeking false pleasure to secure the pain.
All in time fading away.
The seed was never nurtured so it died
It was aborted before it had a chance to grow.
Tainted with assumptions and deception.
Forfeited the balance of inception.
Now this triggered the tower
Broken cords bond by pricking the scabs.
Convicted flames burn up the porch in rage.
Someone will aim but no one will escape the game

Night Sweats

For every time you cried puddles of tears on that pillow
Yet and still, you awakened from the omission of sorrow
Shackled with imprisonment enduring this shame
Head held high walking through empty corridors.
Heart so heavy from frivolous actions
Couldn't even breathe yet you soared.
Still greeting society with a face swollen and soar
All while wrestling demons inside.
Pulling bullet fragments from triggers in your mind
For all those abandoned nights ignorance deceived you
Having withdrawal from codependency
Night terror from inherited cycles
Levitating to unfamiliar places
Hesitating to sleep to keep from seeing familiar faces.
No prayer deep enough to cover the entities lingering in these
spaces.
Floating in darkness relentlessly

Projection

I smile back robotically
Yet, deep down inside there's deficiencies
This thing got a hold on me
I'm silent from the shock of friction transferred to me
The real me screaming from the inconsistencies
Snap out of this
You are thee epitome
But this silent disability has broken places inside of me
I cannot seem to regain
I just need space
Wounded and pierced in the side
It has taken endurance to choose to strive
I can hear the angels say "It's not her time".
Granted another chance at life.
Fresh Wind
Resuscitate
Awaken
Time to begin again.

Spirit to Self

Extending the thought to vent less and pray more
Empowering my inadequate soul to soar
Left standing in the shadows sore
Uttering the words "WHY ME"?

No air, gasping to stay afloat for the rescue.
Taking a leap just to fall from the crash of disappointment.
Trapped in a cloud, silent with emotions.
Building up pressure hoping

Hiding from the mirror
Shadow boxing not for the weak
Got me triggered subconsciously
Peeling layers back to reveal the thieves.
Balance becomes the remedy

<u>8 of Swords</u>

All the hurt in the past.
Struggling to decline the negative thoughts still floating
Protect your portion.
Chant words less distorted
Cycles repeat like reminders.
Choose to exist daily.
Mind stretched from waiting.
Sleeping in chambers
Wolves dress up to kill the sheep.
A prisoner to these thoughts abiding
So distraught by brokenness to see I am free.
LoVe is still the token I seek.

The Way

The heart is no laughing matter
We all want love for bonding mind over matter
Sitting vultures watch and wait
Position your focus on the plate
Cycles of hardship crumble
Let's raise the standard to Logoic
Instead of jumping heart first
Turn off the engine and stall
Exfoliate the mind before you open the vault
Sage too expose the layers of dead weight
Create conversation to exchange
Unveil the vision
Speak it into existence
What is potential without desire
Grab the reign and open the stream
Acknowledge this structure before karma redeems

<u>Nostalgia</u>

Prodigal Being
Prophetic Seer
Premeditating vision with no chaser
Cancel free play in the former days
This gift is none negotible
Blessing them with constant totems
Position wands in dark corridors
Summons clarity inside the storm.
Abstract extension coming from the throne
Strike the rock like Moses felt.
If it's not felt strike it to hell
Stand firm on fable tales.
Dream in the clouds like wishing wells

Baptism

WE get one life inside the ring of grace
Permission granted above the chalice
Confession evokes a dance.
Even with all knowledge
We become submissive to breaking the rules.
Cause deep down inside we rude.
Human nature face is fooled
Running in circles above the water
Washing away fears from the past
After the fast we crash
Chanting quotes of peace stirring the plan.
Breaking shame is not to be silenced.
Release this passion habitually.

Tonic

Stare Into the whole of destiny
Eyes to admire wonder how one sees.
An understanding far beyond deep
An intimate abrasion of a flawless peak
Mysterious figures we all seek.
Empty passion in a cup to fill.
A continuing stage of rage is the appeal.
Hidden secrets we share were real.
Butterflies flutter when your aura is revealed.
Suspicious disagreement then deception appeared.
Created this trap with you forever
Silence tainted the feathers

Foundation

Challenge covenants character to grow beyond the test
Behind the masquerade we confide our deepest sentimemt
Pretending that creation never happened
Once flesh encounters that supernatural experience
It demolishes all doubts
We cannot live without permission
Daily we feel your power radiate
Words spoken die when there is no vibration released
Controlling the source denotes fear
No need patching the wounds
Shed old skin to cover the loins
The spirit will regulate

2 Corinthians 5: 1-8

Dual Perspective

Pendulum swings makes the focus become steady.
Temperance plays friction with praise.
Open mouth speaks plagues resisting the reap
Intercept the pores now seep.
Stretch inside the hallways of unlimited beliefs.
Ego hangs in reverse only to manipulate.
Mixed emotions out of range
Mounting discrepancies in attempt to change
All while standing in the midst of pain.
Only to point fingers in shame
Premature assumptions detained.

Mirror

The Message (Synchronicity)

Simple calculations released in variations
Carrying frequency in its rotation
Remove blockages for clear meditations.
Communicate instructions for spiritual conversations.
Directing signals like aviation
Pressure heats the temple creating different vibrations
Expect elevation
Construct balance in simulation
Counting numbers to see
Calculating factors in sync.
Drifting higher into the light
Wisdom speaks universally.

Purple Haze

Smoke clouds fill spaces in the mind
Penetrate the veil of confessions
Seeking reconcilation from dead connections
Venting beyond manifestation
Find me lighter than the light, that's complexion
Shedding wisdom of traumatic deceptions
Disintegrate words forming in the mind
Nothing seems to define constant imperfections
Divide every concept into confessions
Manipulate the concept until its worthy
Request validation from the shadows
The shift is complicated
Set your eyes on the sparrow
Drifting down this path is narrow
Silence requires no fear
Standing at the peak of regression constantly gripping
This time its me versus me
Walking through the fog naturally
Time to accept the truth
Activate your capacity.

New Exchange

The whole world on edge
Voices whispering invade the air
Brewing up fear taunting instead
Silent enemy unleashed to kill the thread
Digging up myths
Suffocating predications so beware
Setting up church religiously
Fine tuning the key
Running around in circles paying the cost to stay
Constantly building disorders
Stealing the seed
Going crazy just to be reclaimed
All sacrifices aren't created equal

<u>Dizzy Spells</u>

In a dark place disconnected in a daze
Floating through spaces of this reality.
Dizzy from everyone smiling at me
Matching ashes to ashes
Harmonies play frequently in the night.
Standing firm at the shrine
Conflicts matter until midnight.
Concentrated levels consumed.
Finding my way back to the moon
Happiness develops after the storm.
Direct your intentions to the shore.

Run It Back

Running
Racing
Resisting

Trying to beat this ascension.
Premeditate senses now lifted.
Battered by ego's wrath.
Depicting shadows while pacing

Breathing
Bending
Breaking

Accept this sanction
Seeing glitches in layman
Pressure molding to fulfill change.
Carrying light into the spectrum

Ambitious
Acceptance
Aligned

Training life in levels untold
Chasing ripples down the rivers bowl

Breaking branches to hold
Exploring the logic of Edgar's fedora
Wisdom protects the soul

Premonition

There is no perfect resolution
Only a revelation
There is no new me
Only an older self that derives in stealth
The conscious gains vulnerability as levels are built
Recognizing life is perplexed with twisted fate
Bringing unfilitered content to the edge and deflate
Flesh becomes agitated forced to measure intervals in dates
This maze is complicated.
Eyes gazing
Quick compress
Roaming on greener grass that's faking.
Pacing this course awaiting
Touching dimensions
Masked with cold thoughts detaining.
Broken wings from uncharted fables
Stand and receive your privilege

Zero Less Than One

Let's talk about the cycle
Like the deliverers and disciples
This life revolves around
Can I get up?
Can I detach my heart from this broken cup?
Can I suck up the pain of this worlds rain?
Demons devour at you throat making you choke
like a chain
Hatred still remains.
I look down around and all I see is nothing left but half the
link
What did we used to be?
A world that still turns in degrees
No dedication to communicate of what we last seen
Is it all a dream put into motion?
Zombies that think they roam free
To resist the point of thee
Are we free?
Or are we trapped in our own reality?
You can set the time but has time already programmed you
Every day I look around and wonder about the last days
Needless to say, life is already a journey.
As we look around and down upon the zombies.

<u>Power Struggle</u>

Nervous,
Heartbeat racing like out of time
Be quiet until it's aligned.
Ringing bells for change

Life captivates wells in spring
Reading Psalms until the story sings
Manifest billows on cobwebs strings
Heavy burdens from risk not prevailed.

Standing in the heat til' it swells
Overturning the wheel
Embracing character to destroy the rage
Release the diamond in the ruff
Push the clutch out of stagnation.
Drag them bags into the fire
Let the smoke clear

3:33 AM

There are no mistakes.
For your life the divine orchestrated restraints
Now it begins,
Awake
The tower crumbles.
Swinging swords no aim
New beginnings are paced.
Steady shaking
Vibrating
Mirror gazing
No hating
Destroyed by abandonment.
Juxtaposed and complacent
Contradicting character
Protect the seal
While holding lilies in favor of the wheel.
The promise can still be obtained
It's time to remember your're Ancient . (A-Chent)

Unmerited Favor

No signature required
This condition freely given
Suffering is necessary for what is written
Committed to walk, adhere and listen
Laying the bricks one by one
Strength required to cheer
Transforming wisdom from the deer
Wrapped in all black to steer
Spinning circles in the forest
Billows haunting to elate the doom
Carrying them down to the cupboard
Mixing until the ingredients are consistent.

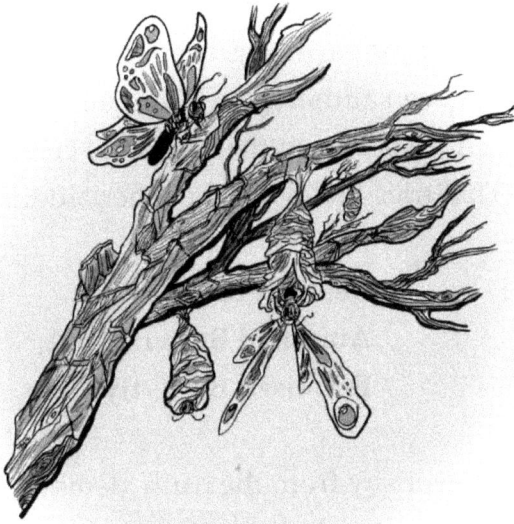

Transformation

Promised Butterfly

Created before the earth was ever spoken into existence.
Given authority to lead a mission.
A jar of clay at the bottom of creed,
That tries to devour the inherited faith.

Beautiful Butterfly
Anointed Butterfly
Promised Butterfly

Never shy from the truth, demand it
Prepare to take your place in kingship
You are majesty, created to serve
Without hesitation bloom your power

Beautiful Butterfly
Anointed Butterfly
Promised Butterfly

To know your identity is far from insanity

Stay hidden in the depth of truth
Release the past
Be one with your magic, let it be your guiding light

Beautiful Butterfly
Anointed Butterfly
You're the Promised Butterfly
Fly High!

Dedicated to "Aunt Geraldine" thank you for this gift!

<u>The Word Love</u>

I'm sitting here thinking about the word we call LOVE.
And what it means when it comes directly from above
First Love was a choice a plan decision from the beginning.
This word goes deeper than the mouth it impresses the heart.
Then its truth leaves no room for doubt
Then it destroys all Imagination, dreams and thoughts of
LOVE.
I'll never know how much it cost to SEE my sin upon the
rugged cross.
It's crazy how it bought me out of captivate, bitterness and
unforgiveness.
My spiritual appetite for you is overacted aint it amazing.
How you preserve my life so I can praise your name forever
Your worthy
God without you , where would I be?
I'd be just another reflection of my ancestor you SEE
I decided not to go down that same road and pay that same
toll
I refuse to live my life as another extension of sin unrepented.
I refuse to pass on a legacy of ignorance.
Yet, in spite of the stall, you loved me flaws and ALL
Then you showed me I'm worthy of love beyond my faults
Which forced me to SEE that the word love is

Action and when put into practice can change anyone person,
place or thing
That's how you SEE me.

Love

Draw Nigh

Break Away
Lying cold on a dormant slate
Equally scared but anxious for fate
Starring into the superconscious now mink
Ready for the anchor to go further in deep.

Come Stay
Dive anxiously into this wave
Vibrations shake the foundation to awake.
As heavy rain pours to cleanse the pores.
Evoking the heart to explore .

Stay Away
From untamed pastures
Building boundaries against imposters.
Spreading chains like good luck charmers
Floating naked down the stream of armor

Fade Away
It seems.
Never to return and seek
Alone to grieve.
This is my fallacy

<u>The Stirring</u>

Often the question is what is my purpose?
Why am I here?
With an anxious heart full of anxiety
We shake the crystal ball waiting for the answer to appear.
Not knowing that superficial obstacles are near, Hovering like
a drone
The day God whispered your name into your mother's womb.
Creation begins to define molecular hues
Purpose ignited passion to delegate this journey.
Through design his power urgently displayed
Engineered with desire but eventually reshaped.
From distractions absorbed in range
Obsessed with being portrayed.
We have forgotten real connections.
Drowning by envy, lust, and personal perfections
With every host presented
Our image is tainted.
No one cares about true intentions.
Speaking to the death, that is gifted.
Now the hidden figures are in the distance

<u>Hourglass</u>

Soothing the atmosphere realistically
Centerpieces displayed endlessly.
Knowing that my heart is sincere.
Options are few and near.
Voices speaking together clear.
Silent from fear
Every object appears.
Sudden shock upon confessions
Lead bleeding hearts into intercession
Magnify the need for blessings.
Lessons reset continue to oppress.
Change becomes infected.
How can I be effective?

Day Vision

Even in the depth of perception
The challenge to comprehend has been predestined.
What provides you with passion
Even when it's not all picture perfect
The sanity is distorted.
Abused by anxiety
These thoughts arrest me
Stopping the flow of sanctity
I am a prisoner to my innergy
Ambition becomes the enemy.
As I hesitate through my own infatuations
My qualities evolve inadequately.
Then I denigrate back to the old me
Requesting old receipts
Haunting principles of relentless things
Shooting daggers for debates
Just wait
Anything left blinking is hazardous.
Look beyond the patches
Create freedom in stashes
Lay to rest the matches
Love until its passive

Intermission

Am I wrong for having a free will of knowledge to trust the
worth of those who forsaken me?
Intimidate me with other self-worth
I am the 6,000 reconciliated birth.
Impersonate my mind but don't insult my intelligence.
I am the image of my father's chosen breed
My integrity is far more than this life can array.
Still optimum when their deceptive to me
But none can match this synergy.
All eyes on the one who loves me.
Step into the battle zone
This is spiritual warfare.
True plagues of demonic energy
Let me rephrase
What thought's will be omited?
Agonizing from a distant
The greatest creation is your own dimension.
Time for an Intermission
Make them all convert.
Magician!

Green Revival

I am a pillar of hope
Trust in love like lending a hand
Sweet nectars bond for cleansing & care
Be of good cheer even when your dared

I choose to be visible
Be an example for change
Show that vulnerability can still relate
Serve with boundaries of compassion

I forgive myself, as I forgive others
Evaluate the egos intentions daily
Be willing to see the phase
Trust the alchemy being exchange

Phoenix Prophecy

Set fire like an unpredictable blaze
No match can measure this majesty.
Like the sun, moon, and the stars that's creativity.
His power like the vortex on the inside of me
So endless, it reinvents the pedigree.
Your existence is legendary.
Darkness cannot defeat its magnitude is never ending.
One experience in his presence
Makes hearts beat new rhythm.
Carry this as your atonement.
Remain buried at the root.
My stature is concrete in his truth.
I am Free, I am One.
Once dehydrated now my thirst for him saturates the shame
In this place my position is reclaimed

<u>Anchored</u>

Just like a raging water
I stand at the edge of the boarder.
There I'm battling with my faint subconscious daughter.
Trying to break this curse of generational order.
Yes, I know that I am CHOSEN.
But these thoughts in my mind are frozen.
So comfortable I fall back into the daily buzz
Instead of fighting for a fresh word.
Now I'm average by statics.
Instead of depending on TRUTH.
I leaned on a quick fix and it faded before me.
The open record of doubt is detached, and it must be closed.
Before I soon lose
All of who you told me I'd be
So I got to BELIEVE
"what's that "
I gotta believe that Im more than what I see in the mirror.
It's clearer that my heart was wicked.
God I needed you nearer
So many voices I hear.
But only yours matters.
Shattering all that chattering like glass
Because in the past I would have BUST you
But now I thank God because I trust you

To bring me through every situation
I will always believe that's its you who's leading.
Even though my heart is bleeding.
I would never manipulate the system.
As I recognize that's it's YOU who 's been, keeping ME!!!

Peace

I Am She

Subliminal Goddess
Master of Opposition
Silent from within
Daily you become resilient.
Opening new doors to see your worth.
Limitless to the barrier
Destined for greatness.
Found peace within creative spaces.
Wading deep beyond the waves
Diving in purpose for humanity.
Accepting the gift of sanity
Rebirth is your remedy .

Father

Arise with all power from the sky.
Light shining bright no disguise
Absorbing my reasoning, Why?
Illuminating my affliction too shine
Like the spirit of the raven
Displaying the strength of a thousand men
Teaching lesson in sunrays
Guiding this vessel through perceptions
Protect wisdom on higher ground
Providing logic to my brain
Setting this soul, aflame
Content in this new restraint
Grateful for the new day!

<u>Rooted Deep</u>

Your perspective will not bind my intelligence
This message is receptive.
Love and Peace means protected.
Be patient and choose the best inception
Earned foundations give aliment to the seeker
Do not apologize for masculine aggression.
Being left in limbo breeds misery
Stay in balance that's intimacy
Trees deep rooted display their history
Wrapped in vines that stay persistant
Sacred lesson planted by the elders
Wells run dry from trauma bonding.
Follow the urge of your soul
There is Inhertiance
Embrace the Legacy
Draw back the arrow of strength
If I cease to fight for my truth than I am just an illusion.

<u>Crowned</u>

Saturated in frankincense and myrrh.
Dripping self-love to the core
Buried deep in this transition
What I needed is needing me to listen
Open my mouth only to speak blessings
Send light to anyone seeking to be free
These shadows resemble people like me
Lurking in spaces in between
Talking rough to appear to be complete
Chase the good only to be disappoint in siege
Repetition is only for the mystique
Remembrance activates those who BElieve

Love Is Transcending

Infatuated with infatuation.

Love can be obsessive.

Like a record it's in heavy rotation

The master plan is Loyalty with No sanctions

It can flow in abundance or be guarded at the gate.

The mindset determines its fate.

It can be a fit a rage or mink like grace.

The foundation of the human experience in this life is high rate of

expectancy

It's an acquired taste, often displayed in time and space.

With 3 words the cycles of hurt, pain and fear can be restored

Longing for sincere dimensions

In open spaces fate awaits

Bow in a submissive state.

For the value of love, cherish it relentlessly.

Creating connections so powerful generations rule for centuries

Turn obstacles from illusions into reality.

Embody passion so deep it burst from the core

An opposition without direction internally deplete it.

In order to keep the flow, you must surrender

over and over again

Not just at the pivotal point of the commitment

The sacrifice must be a repeated ascension.

Let's become embedded in your soul
Love is transcending.

Legacy (ELW)

Evolved from the
Running of their blood
In my life
Keeping the enemies under my feet
And the authority to make them flee

Laboring in the dark
Acknowledging
The truth in the light
Anticipating the cost
Standing strong
Honoring the love ones lost in the night
Ancient warrior of life

Wind in the harvest that
Hums to the grains
Identifying my presence
That the rain has softly went away
Although you can only feel me
Keep growing so that I can blow your seeds away
Evolved from your ancestors
Reunited through the veins

M Three

Deep within my core
Burrowed the seeds of 3.
A messengers of wisdom , A protector and warrior of strength
My replica of trinity
Wrapped deep in geometry.
From the frequency of divinity
Life flourished from inside of me.
They call me
"Divine Mother"
Transcending from dimensions
The depth of my why now revealed.
When they questioned my integrity
In this portal my 3 will inspire humanity
Their very existence will advocate my name.
That I was destined for greatness despite the suffering
I decree that they will see no oppositions
Total access within distant realms
Invested into the highest currency called Love.
From the blood flowing in this immortal
They are my legacy.

Dedicated to my 3 beautiful children.
Thank you for choosing me to be your "Divine Mother".
I love you deeply!

The Mantle

Purposely redefining opposition to enlighten your journey.
That's example.
Running this race
Holding the torch
Like a mantle
Readjusting the lens
That's focus
My desire is for
Everyone to live in their purpose.
That's Hoping
Providing wisdom from experience
To help you cope
Yet Prophetic dreams haunting
Dearly Beloved
Time is shifting.
There is no space for halting.
Pendulums Shaking
Foundations breaking
New Regime
Eyed wide open

<u>Mother</u>

The moon is full.
My body is aligned.
Confessing my intentions into the night
Transforming these demons into the light
Burdens once formed are cryptic messages now clear.
Feeling my purpose begin to flare.
Decision making creates clarity.
Hidden truths enlightened mine eyes.
Exalt the source as it nurtures despair.
Console me with your tender energy here.
Guide my soul through these phases.
Lift me up into your gaze
Calm this anxious heart filled with shame.
Flow within the sacred touch of her rays.

The Gift

Sometimes it's bigger than you
So, let it overtake you
Ride this wave fully awakened
Listen deep within shackles breaking
Freedom is endless when its in your mind
My focus is abundance
No money can satisfy
I surrender to the divine
Dance until I'm aligned
My name is phoenix, rose from the ashes, warrior, free spirit
I'm the generational curse breaker
You say anything less and that's low vibrational
I stand in the dark spaces for those vindicated
We reign, so let's reciprocate it
If you still focus on the material
I can't relate
This next war spiritual
My dreams are visual
My thoughts are critical
My words are powerful
Everything for me is reachable my children teachable
Passing through many lifetimes and still come out pure as
gold
Where I go when I pass from this life

Only God knows
I want to leave a lasting impression.
But that starts from within me
Where dark and light collide
Every choice causes a sequence to arise
Surrender to the flow in order to grow.
Only God knows the purpose that we hold.
Everything that we need is on the inside of our soul.

ABOUT THE AUTHOR

ELW (A-Chent) is a poet, Shamanic life coach, Hypnotherapy Practitioner. EFT/TFT Master practitioner and all experienced lightworker with intuitive abilities. She also has a Bachelor's degree in Human Services from (ODU) . A Domestic Violence survivor who gained the desire to help others just like herself overcome adversity and challenges. She began her career volunteering and working in various local shelters too working as a facilitator for various support groups then transitioning as a Case Manager/ QMHP working with adults with disabilities within her community.

Insomnia of a little girl which tells the transformative journey through the process of ending deep rooted trauma too self-mastery into rebirth. ELW (A-Chent) speaks of the uncomfortable journey of releasing the spiritual ties from pain within self. She deeply provides insight while encouraging others to "Feel" the transformation. This poetic collection will bring healing and strength to those who have been stagnant, fearful, and feeling unworthy.

Darkness should not be feared but embraced because it pushes our light to shine from behind the shadow. It your perspective!!

Know that YOU are the most powerful tools you have access to in life. Use it wisely!

www.ingramcontent.com/pod-product-compliance
Lightning Source LLC
Chambersburg PA
CBHW060704030426
42337CB00017B/2764